# Before the War

*poems as they happened*

Lawson Fusao Inada

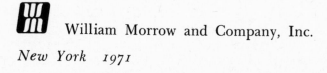 William Morrow and Company, Inc.

*New York 1971*

For my love, Janet

Some of these poems first appeared in *Aion* (Asian American Political Alliance), *The Carleton Miscellany, Chicago Review, Evergreen Review, Kayak, Quixote,* and *United Church Herald.*

"Bandstand" and "R and R in Bangkok" appeared in *3 Northwest Poets,* Quixote Press, 1970.

Special acknowledgment *must* be made here to those without whose strength and continual inspiration this volume would not have been possible. Among them: Clifford Brown, John Coltrane, Miles Davis, Billie Holiday, Milt Jackson, Charlie Parker, Bud Powell, Sonny Stitt, and Lester Young.

# Contents

## Coming into Oregon

## Don't Know

## The Stand

*Plucking Out
a Rhythm*

# Plucking Out a Rhythm

Start with a simple room—
a dullish color—
and draw the one shade down.
Hot plate. Bed.
Little phonograph in a corner.

Put in a single figure—
medium weight and height—
but oversize, as a child might.

The features must be Japanese.

Then stack a black pompadour on,
and let the eyes
slide behind a night of glass.

The figure is in disguise:

slim green suit
for posturing on a bandstand,
the turned-up shoes of Harlem  . . .

Then start the music playing—
thick jazz, strong jazz—

and notice that the figure
comes to life:

sweating, growling
over an imaginary bass—
plucking out a rhythm—
as the music rises and the room is full,
exuding with that rhythm  . . .

Then have the shade flap up
and daylight catch him
frozen in that pose

as it starts to snow—
thick snow, strong snow—

blowing in the window
while the music quiets,
the room is slowly covered,

and the figure is completely
out of sight.

# From Our Album

*I. "Before the War"*

"Before the war"
means Fresno, a hedged-in house,
two dogs in the family.

Blackie, the small one, mine,
lapped at his insides
on the floorboard, on the way to the doctor.

Jimmy, my father's shepherd,
wouldn't eat after the evacuation.
He wouldn't live with another master

and pined away, skin and bone.

With feelings more than pride,
we call him our one-man dog.

## II. Mud

Mud in the barracks—
a muddy room, a chamber pot.

Mud in the moats
around each barracks group.

Mud on the shoes
trudging to the mess hall.

Mud in the swamp
where the men chopped wood.

Mud on the guts
under a loaded wagon—

crushed in the mud by the wheel.

## III. Desert Songs

### 1. ALL THAT WE GATHERED

Because there was little else to do,
they led us to the artillery range
for shells, all that we gathered,
and let us dig among dunes
for slugs, when they were through.

Because there was little else to do,
one of them chased a stray
with his tail between his legs
and shot him through the head.

### 2. SHELLS

A desert tortoise—
something mute and hard—

something to decorate
a desert Japanese garden:

gnarled wood, smooth
artillery shells for a border.

When a guard
smashes one, the shell

cracks open and the muscles ooze.

### 3. IT IS ONLY NATURAL

The pheasant is an Oriental creature,
so it is only natural
that one should fly into camp

and, famished by rations and cans,
break out in secret, native dance
over a fire, on a black coal stove.

### 4. SONG OF THE 442ND

Caged creatures
have curious moods.

Some of them choose
to be turned

loose in a group,
to take their chances

in the open.

### 5. STEERS

Because a dentist
logically drives a butcher truck,

I rode with my father
to the slaughterhouse on an afternoon.

Not hammers, not bullets,
could make him close his eyes.

### 6. HE TEACHES

He jerks the eyes
from birds, feet
from lizards,

and punishes
ants with the gaze
of a glass.

And with his sly
gaze, his child's face,
he teaches

what has its place,
and must be
passed on to others.

## IV. Song of Chicago

When the threat lessened,
when we became tame,
my father and friends
took a train to Chicago

for factory work,
for packaging bolts.
One grew a mustache
and called himself Carlos.

And they all made a home
with those of their own—

rats, bedbugs, blacks.

# Father of My Father

For Mitsuji Inada

The way the incense gripped,
coughing, everyone coughing,
their throats resounding in the hall . . .

Above the stage, a dragon
licked his lip.

They were moaning, bowing and moaning—
three old-kimonoed men,
their tassels flapping.

The altar bristled
lacquer and gold latches.

Then clapping wood, the gift
of incense to the bowl . . .


2.

Incense. Sucking the wind from him—
face a deflated callus . . .

Then the shoes paraded, on and on,
issuing from the walls.

Finally, to be strolling
over the garden—

gaunt rocks, bonsai
knuckled at the bottom.

About, all structures
surrounding the pagoda of San Jose.


3.

Have you ever seen
blue eyes in a Japanese face?

That is the main thing I remember.

She took the wrong road
nightly at their intersection,
leaving him shouting, screaming,
pacing the house with a flashlight

as if something was missing.

Have you ever lost your woman?
Have you ever lost your crops
and had to move?—
packing up without your woman,
some evacuation going on . . .

Have you ever been wakened
by blue eyes shining into your face?

You wondered who you were.

You couldn't move.

*4.*

Or there were evenings
steeped in scrolls and incense  . . .

Sometimes, to be alone
in that museum, cleaved
by shadows, the tongue's disfigurings  . . .

In Arkansas he staked a ragged garden.
Then that Colorado wind
eroded.

I flourished in that sand.

But what comes second-hand
is not the same.

Something is missing.

I sometimes wake to streetlight
pacing in my room.

I would not hold him then.

Nothing could stop me now.

*Into the Open*

# In a Storm

Late afternoon, and the grove
snaps under weight of snow.
Their bodies cannot bear
such extension,

the force that makes them
more than they are:

branches have broken;
one whole tree
goes groping like a squid.

We have barely met.

We talk a little, share
a short, dry kiss,

then go on talking—

and each word said
brings snow and branches down upon us.


2.

Night, and another snow:
dense, wafting,
all but stopping in descent.

We have been captive
to its fancies:

rolling, floating in a drift.

Now the walls have us:
shapes that might be
Joshuas on a mesa praising rain.

But cold, heat come
flowing out of darkness

in a storm we make.

# Into the Open

*I.*

I found you red-hooded
in the forest of a city,
purse as big as a basket.

Your grandmother was dead.
Another you loved had left.

Here, where I live,

hoods and all that gruff
exterior come down to skin.

No one can come in.

## II.

What is in that basket?—

notes of a bad love,
a delinquent address.

I've the same in my bin—

records going back
to some calamitous setting—

Miles muting all blues,
time to go home.

What good is the past
if you can't use it?

Let us play the music.

No one is absent.

We are all the loves we ever lost.

*III.*

This is the house of castoffs,

where they are allowed to gather,

grooving the music
local jukeboxes cannot hold.

This is the house of midnight creepers—

tracks of pom-poms in the snow
from a clandestine convertible.

This is the house across the station—

where night sticks never sleep.

You are sleeping.

Bud Powell chases rainbows.

*IV.*

Let me serve something to you.

Here, this juice
has been extracted from soybeans—

steeped in brine, fermenting.

These greens come down
from Waterloo—

smuggled out of the South
when they escaped by rail.

Try them. Taste.

One of these days
we'll have to make something

together, sweet.

*V.*

This space that I claim,
this opening from chest to elbow—

what is it for?

Waking, my right arm
throbbing a tune in my ear,

humming the not quite pain
of adjustment and growth,

I find what should have been there,
where nothing was before.

# Folk  Song  for  Janet

It would be pure:

essence of lullaby
hummed to a child
in the upper
reaches of Appalachia—
the valley sleeping,
night reclining
over the mine's encroachment;

and some of the blues
out of Houston,
traded between men
in a cage, for tickets
on the midnight train;

and bits of the cowman's tune,
alone and strumming
to a cactus, cows at grass
under a scavenger's moon;

and the jazzman's mood,
filtered through a mute
to bad glass
gathering at his feet—
what he must dwell upon;

and out of these, the song
all lovers sing—
all feeling—with night sea

lulling, covering them.

*Utica,*
*North Platte*

# The Source

Bare
hills, cross-
legged, brush
in the folds
moist
into summer
and the drought.
Rivers
are cold.
Sand,
too hot
to hold
gives
to my motion.
Hawks
in the sky—
something
burnt
and floating.

Carrion is dry
stuff
gleaned
of essential.
You are
where
postmen rarely
tread.
Dry things,
and rivers
running
hurriedly
from the source.

# Disease

Circumstance
and ripped tickets
bring us here;
chewing gum sticks
us in place.

I do not know him.

This is his
country: crop dusters,
vultures; horses,
mute police cars  . . .

A sick fish, wet-
eyed, slits
in his windpipe  . . .

Night under sea,
light rippling by.

I do not sleep.

I try.

Shirtless, he
floats the aisle—
scales for eyes,
gills in his chest.

He kisses me.

I die.

I will not breathe.

# Utica, North Platte

Take any flat, plain piece of land,
give it a name—
Utica, North Platte—
motels take shape around the syllables.
Some movie screens . . .

You come and register, sick
with the edges,
furtive dog among the brushes . . .

The scent of flesh,
of lovers' luggage,
the crushed mosquito's image . . .

The city has her window open—
bugs cluster at the screen.
She shoves and tugs her silent lover . . .

Night of tall doors
opening for truckers, some bitch within . . .

Then to be a convict,
on the run,
licenses and whiskey sagging the back end . . .

Someone tugs the covers from you.
Tracing the edges,
you are about to cry . . .

By morning she is tired and sleeping—
window white, closed . . .

The night has grown
metallic flowers in her garden—

straight and hard,
all of the same color.

# Let Me

One is a range of mange that fells the hair,
leaving wrinkles and spots like a man.
What mange leaves, the ticks take,
puffed thick as pebbles on a riverbed.

The other is a sea of fleas, worms
breaking surface like dolphins
dipping in that twitching sea.

These are the dog and cat. Scrape them,
they pop and smear but never scream:
they are beyond that, lounging on a porch
of splinters—gargoyles at the portal.

Dinner is over.
Platters slap into stacks amidst the hum
of women, the cattle moving barnward with the men.

A child's moon haunts the sky.

Over the field the lean bats fly.
And fireflies. They were like flak upon my shield.

Grandfather, let me fondle Babe and Mike.
Peel me bare and let the big June beetle
nuzzle me, the black-eyed dragonfly.

Let me love.

# The Way I Came

Behind, from where I came,
houses, white and quiet,
kept me on my way.
Like graves, I would not
pry among them, moon and darkness
flattening them to placards,
with darkness out behind.

But here, a road
rolls onward as a belt,
conveying lovers to their bed,
others sleeping in the melancholy
of ended visits, stiff-necked,
oblivious, as an old man drives.

And somewhere there is music,
little more than sound.
But it *is* music,
within the sound
of traffic, the cattle
moaning into Illinois.

Soon, a figure
moans and lurches in a daze
of pen and stain—

noisy, the way he came.

*In These*
*Encounters*

# Children of Somersworth

Heading north against the grain
of birds following
mills long gone to Alabama,
rocks a harvest, hills
used up and over,
houses, car hulls, rusting . . .

The Salmon Falls River
is a larva pool, full
of detergent.
Power poles pray like mantes.

Somersworth almost died.
It sucked in some praying
Canucks, shoe factories,
the bad breath of a tannery.

Factory tenements
brace the eyeteeth of spires.

Children are women and men.
Feed books to them.
They sleep. They drool.

This morning, blue as the pool,
we saw huge antennas
sucking and drooling
on the scabby roofs
of the sleeping
children of Somersworth.

# Hunters

set out from South America
southward past its gruff, swept tips
until the land
loses itself in water, wild water,
crumpling into squalls, coming down in black
for days without relenting  . . .

Then water, wind, surrender into blues,
white banners
puff and flatten in the breeze
as if to barter with the beauty of lagoons,
pure moods of snow
where penguins totter up in supplication,
seals dip and slide  . . .

Past all this the hunters glide:

honed herd and a mother
floating factory decked out in artillery—
what was used on Guadalcanal  . . .

This Sunday, grace still ringing,
as you settle with your family to the food—

whale steaks, whale soup—

in your scrumptious whale suit,
tell me, is it good?

Is it good?


    2.

I saw the hunters moving to the kill  . . .

And when the lead bull fell,
the herd
chose not to run,
bobbing about the bull as if to buoy him up,
as if to save him somehow
from what struck them all to slow,
mute writhing . . .

And blood was all there was
to mingle with the sea; icebergs in the distance
northward bound to their own destruction—

sullen, dripping grief . . .


    3.

Here, in Maine, there is no whaling.

This is no deterrent for the hunters
cutting by to still the raging deer
who take salt from my land.

Something like a bomb
to find him in his shelter.

Or a civil hate.

Or that hunter's patience,
bobbing up one explosive noon
to take the newsboy from his bicycle—

faceless, bloating, unraveling
with the print of highway death and drowning  . . .


    *4.*

I am plagued by birds,
the city in my barn.

And woodchucks, squirrels  . . .

Even my own small cat, wobbly as a tripod,
waking from his daily sleep
to ask where shot legs go, and why,
as if I were some lord of balance—

too weak to snuff him away  . . .

Once, out of Amarillo,
head in a dream, foot down in passing gear,
a dog appeared—

an ordinary dog, brown  . . .

There was no time for stalking, savoring;
there was no time for anything
but a dog's dying—

such hard, gold headlights of eyes—

no time except for one short backward glance
at a broken, flapping mass

before I hunted on.

# In These Encounters

Mousie, three-legged cat,
hears me coming, yawns,
turns upon his back
and turns again to sleep.

Janet, on the same bed,
doesn't even hear me,
twisted in sleep beneath
today's schoolpapers,
dreaming for snow,
buses snarled in drifts . . .

I had been sketching below,
shaping a soul
to spread on the blackboard
tomorrow, a day of the year.

I had one crying today.
I thought his arm would break
as I gripped it to the bone.
I thought his face would rip.
I thought my soul would break
long after he was gone.

In these encounters:
this is how we exist.

Come, sun, uncover us
in a drift. We are ready

to be ripped open and devoured.

# Wintersong

For Bill Evans


Suspended from the eaves
the feeder swings, cold
plastic pagoda brimmed
with seeds the wind flings
scattering in the snow.
Beyond those low
eaves, the frozen teeth,
are juncos in the trees.
Trees too thin for snow
and three birds weaving
wintersong among them—
music on a sheet.
Music eased by one
alone, from a piano,
brooding over the keys,
holding each note
for all its worth,
alone and whole  . . .

When the flourish goes,
emptiness comes, space
of fields simplified
by snow, that between
note and other note,
unreckoned with before.
That which differentiates

lasting deed from forage,
the mindless bickerings  . . .

Noon on the kitchen clock.
The mail truck stops
and skitters in the road.
Coming from the box,
I consider the irony
of the house—modern,
spare as any feeder,
the owner somewhere
in Florida—and, caught
once more in the snow,
with stuff disposed of
by the postman—notes
and cancelings from
San Francisco—I know
whatever juncos know.

# The Cloisters as Memory

What I remember: frozen
stone on frozen sole.
Clutter like the streets below:
trinkets for Christmas,
the profusion of one who droops by the hour—
strung out like so many flowers.
And the unicorn's capture:
plums and guts in the weaver's sequence
with lint from his coat,
skin from his fingers
meshed with the unicorn in his threaded fence.

Those nobles—
what did they say?—
strapped in their caskets,
X's by their names like kisses  . . .

And, coming in on the Hudson,
a lone tug lofted its prow like an old weapon
chopping at water,
trailing a thin wake tickling Manhattan,
the electrical storm that was Jersey,
where, on the Palisades,
a caravan of trees paused in a parade
undone—hard rain flogging it all
to crepe, tissue, the remains of wire . . .

Then lightning touched the evening
like a wand, and conversation was a prayer
for Man—

the all that we are,
what we have become.

# Blue Gene

Put another nickel in
Gene Ammons, down
at his heels, in the bottom
of his day. See him sway,
the juice come
sluicing out from
last year's lean, flux
of flab and splintered reeds.

Blow it, Gene.

Tell it, Gene. Tell me
what the owner told me—
gestures of the dazed
connections, sleepless,
planing in from Chi.

Tell me, Gene. Tell me
what you couldn't tell me
in that freezing room, fly
down, vomit on the bowl,
drops around your eyes
like stuff from wounds.

Blue Gene and those
blue-green mallards
in the river ice outside—

singing and singing in the night.

# Thresher

corncob  lobster leg
three mildewed leaves
nail  drain  stain
of evaporating snow
branch  shadow
and loose glass here
all on an asphalt pier

below a bridge
above the sea
I sense the strength
of a fly  the steamer's weakness
whooning in among the
shipyard drum and scream

there is no sun  yet
sweat denies that
iron bench on gabardine
leather on my feet
how to contend with these

snow  april  spring
a walking man with
diamond ring  No
a hook for a hand
whistling  I do not know
the tune  this
is dis jointed limb   hands
feeling  piecing together
glass  cob  broken
nail around a drain
on shadowed asphalt
over       No

and water  governing
so much sand
shudders   allowing us to see
eels that are weeds

help me  help me

# Images of a Day, Congealed

Nothing eventful. From noon
waking and the warm cocoa
warming us within, sweet,
you across our kitchen table
in your checked red duster
and your dark hair down;
chickadees on the feeder
sleeker with the snow
gone, clearing the meadow,
the new colors coming in  . . .

And what an awareness of trees,
their fists of leafings,
as we watched white islands
skimming toward the sea.

At dusk, casual couples
pirouetted where drifts had been,
sharing remnants of the sun
and that white ball
floating high above the nets
in quiet lobbings, softly,
and softly, as a white ball,
came the April moon.

Then we were home again,
tuning the radio in a game.

Across the continent, night,
melancholy, from Fort Wayne.

Sleepily, fading
in and out with the radio,
you remembered that drive
some time ago, unable
to say exactly *why*
we were driving, except
that it was also spring
and a corrugated hut
in a high country clearing
caught our eye, and we noted it,
for remembering.

Nothing eventful since then.
Nothing eventful today. Surely
goodness and mercy will follow us
all the days of our life.

# Cathedral

Shall I say I had a premonition?
Something in the wind?
Something half-expected, certainly,
entering the Province,
mouthing the inflection of the customs man.

What could I do but nod?

Then to be without smooth
roads razored through the stubble,
the stunted towns and logjams
that are central Maine, dropping
into ruts, signs beyond translation,
fields terraced to the streams  .  .  .

And always, in the midst of these,
a church, gleaming in a field, silver
roof and spire radiating  .  .  .

One could not turn away:

the reach of silver
reflecting off the farmyards
in a clear connection.

2.

All to Quebec it was the same.

And where towns had come, buildings
buttressed to that structure.

Sunlight striking
silver in the scythes toppling
grass for horse-drawn carts to gather  . . .

3.

Then black bluffs
rocking from a toll boat.
The jagged city shaking
silver rain

as all bells tolled.

Raveled at the tongue,
scrambling
up the bluffs and by the walls,

stubbing my feet on cobblestones  . . .

4.

And so I stumbled to Beaupré.

Sunlight on the river plain
silver at Beaupré.

Sunlight on the braces
silver at Beaupré.

Sunlight on the altar
silver at Beaupré.

Sunlight on the healing waters
silver at Beaupré.

And at the mass they plummeted
again and again  . . .

Shall I say
I found the ritual fitting?

Shall I say
I found the chanting
logical and simple as a cross?

I only know
that walking with the masses into the sun,
the spires were braces
raised into the sun.

I only know
that gazing over the silver seaway,

that water seemed not to wide to cross.

*Coming into*
*Oregon*

# Coming into Oregon

. . . So there I was,
cruising, evergreen
waving her negligee, moon
a hallway light
ushering me in . . .

Come sunlight, I was
crushed to culverts
by runaway
trucks strapped to logs . . .

That wasn't all:

past the hall
of tresses, clumps
of bad skin glowered through—

gouges of the grizzly's
awful claw—

disheveled flesh,
the ruptured follicles . . .

And in the old
unhealed places, machinery
at the folds like gnats  . . .

That man who invented logging  . . .

I'm going to have his mother
for an evening—

him listening in the hall—

then let him in
come morning, to hush
and soothe her, try
to brush and smooth her over  . . .

Yeah.

# Blues for Dan Morin

*I.*

OK, for October.
People keep screaming
about rain.
Shirtless, I sprawl on grass
looking down a sky-well,
clouds on top like foam.

You are gone in foam.

And all about this development
they're readying themselves for rain:

storm doors snapping into place,
the rasp of rakes  . . .
Someone snips a lawn
for the last time.

And that flicker?—

he's at it still.
If he's not careful he'll
split his bill
breaking into my attic.

What creatures won't do
for winter.

And you, you
slipped off Fire Island and
drowned.

And since July, I've been
lying around.

And I say *let*
the rain come.
I've got wet
anguish in my throat.

And like the sawmill soot,
I'm burnt, funky, diffuse  .  .  .

But when I get
inside, I bust and bust

my head against the wall.

*II.*

Man
I feel
ridiculous

scuttling through
suburbia
on a skinny

tired bike
with gears going
tick tick tick

and dinner doors
closing and kids
going

in and it
getting
dusk

on me
tick tick
and I

don't dig
it  being
outside

Morin  we
were friends
I mean

your dying  it's
a bitch
a drag

I mean it's
taking two
bites

out of a
melon turning
around

one time
and finding
nothing but

rind rind rind

*III.*

I am thinking of one
who would save life,
like a favorite record,
to keep it from wearing.

One who has let another
pass, biding his time,
who would walk all night
now, through the snow.

I am thinking of one
who *was* music, orchestra
strength, unencumbered,
trumpet cutting to bone.

One who walked in snow
for music, whose insight
another would shy from,
misfortune make absurd.

I am thinking of one
who has his collection
of records, all caught
on the cacophony of waste,

of what cannot be heard.

*IV.*

"Una Muy Bonita"
    —Ornette Coleman

Might as well
sing something
softly to myself, some
Bird thing tripped
quickly off the tongue,
percolator bass,
typewriter
drum like the flicker
gone to my head now, deep
in the attic,
tapping and humming  . . .

Might as well
sing something
on the phonograph, blowing
rings around a Spanish tune,
melodious
smoke like lace
pervasiveness of fog
lifting now,
above the Cascades  . . .

Might as well
sing and type, thinking
of two now gone:
one anonymous as fog,
the other in some
impossible exile,
drifting through Europe
with a self-tuned violin  . . .

Might as well
sing and watch the sun rise—
smoke, fog, music
dispersing
over the heater's shiver,
the field frost's grip and snap  . . .

Might as well.
Might as well.

Mist hymn.
The hissing shingle.

Might as well.
Might as well.

Creek crack.
The ringing ripple.

Might as well.
Might as well.

Weed chant.
The clinking field.

Might as well.
Might as well.

Beak clack.
The tinking wheel.

Might as well.
Might as well.

Sun hum muscle
strum mountain
drum roaring
orbit Ornette Morin

BELLS!

Might as well might as well might as well!

# The Legendary Storm

A legendary storm—that's
what I wanted—a bad
blizzard coming down,
covering me like a legendary
hat—nine big feathers
and a five-inch brim.
That year, we lived in a long house,
eaves like wings, icicle
feathers keeping me in.

This year we've got a cheap flat
with skinny curtains.
The storms come in
when they please.
And there's a big bad bear
snarling around the corner.
He's got a sad face and grey
around his collar.  He's
a mountain;  I'm
me.  Please

send me a child to love.

# Three O'clock

". . . it is always
three o'clock . . ."
—Fitzgerald

## I. Prowler

3 o'clock. Funny
town. Disc jockeys tongue
my ear. Cats
in the gutter.
Nothing
in this town
I want: half-
lit, some fool's plunder,
smothering in a mass
of enema tubes.
Gas
stations, closed.
In Calabama,
pumps
suck oil,
dipping and sucking.
The low moon is
Lady Monroe,
fouled, public,
on a drive-in rack.
Dead. Lovely.
It has come to that.

## II. *Shit*

Someone
flushes a bowl.
Shit.
Suppose
bowls stopped
flushing—
shit
for patios,
walled
high stucco.
Shit
rich with chili,
gathering.
Closets of shit—
my shit,
your shit.
Stores of shit.
Shit
cook-out pits.
Shit roofs,
instant shit.
And it
would be
just like this
town, three
o'clock
in the morning.

### III. Firebirds

Some doors
down—guitars
and sad
faces, young
faces, enflamed
like pickets.

Many doors
away, names like
abbreviations
scream
anthems of
annihilation—
bodies, wicks  . . .

We live in
Stampville,
S & H.
At night, white
creepers
spray the street
like The Great
Extinguisher.

He jives
with matches.
His ass
is in ashes.

All over this world
the sirens are
singing—

Burn Baby Burn.

# Filling the Gap

When Bird died, I didn't mind:
I had things to do—

polish some shoes, practice
a high school cha-cha-cha.

I didn't even know
Clifford was dead:

I must have been
lobbing an oblong ball
beside the gymnasium.

I saw the Lady
right before she died—

dried, brittle
as last year's gardenia.

I let her scratch an autograph.

But not Pres.

Too bugged to boo, I left
as Basie's brass
booted him off the stand
in a sick reunion—

tottering, saxophone
dragging him like a stage-hook.

When I read Dr. Williams'
poem, "Stormy,"
I wrote a letter of love and praise

and didn't mail it.

After he died, it burned my desk
like a delinquent prescription  .  .  .

I don't like to mourn the dead:
what didn't, never will.

And I sometimes feel foolish
staying up late,
trying to squeeze some life
out of books and records,
filling the gaps
between words and notes.

That is why
I rush into our room to find you
mumbling and moaning
in your incoherent performance.

That is why
I rub and squeeze you
and love to hear your
live, alterable cry against my breast.

# Sequence for Janet

### I. Cape Perpetua

Day
trailing her feathers
over the Pacific.
Beaches
swoon, pulling
their covers around them.
I love you,
and it is brandy
to the throat.
A floating
beacon, we light
our own way home.

### II. Webbing

of the afternoon,
everything
stuck to it—
new
mustard weed, old
glass and gravel,
writhing
spring trees
violent with blossom.

Because of that,
some men turn
inside. I turn
to highways
and the web of streets.

Crouched, a thousand eyes,
I come
burning down the string
screaming for beauty
or for grief.

### III. *Never Let It Be Said*

The road divides itself—
all the exits that are Sacramento.

The white lines seek their poles—
neon orbiting itself . . .

The full moon
is in the process of mitosis.

Never let it be said
that I don't love you.

## IV. Defense of Seasons

I think it is lovely that
my love, who
loves greenery, that
odd stuff
poking out of holes,
should have a child
growing within her,
from her own
seed, finding its life
from her soil, her light,
to come up finally
a curled, tendriled thing.

*Don't Know*

# Don't Know

Don't know what's come over me:
like to keep covered up—
flappy caps, and turn away from lights . . .

Thought I was getting somewhere—
the lofty perspective, repose . . .

Here we goes again.

Each morning, cornered by your clicking pens,
I'm the Prince of Articulates
hiccupping in a confessional—

eyes, eyes, eyes . . .

And when mechanics, those
lewd pryers, lift my hood and leer,
I keep my knees closed—

tight, tight . . .

And last night I knew it wasn't right

and I laughed and laughed until I cried.

# Report from the New Country

Say the city is not
stale pastry:

if you know the stack of pies
at the counter's elbow—
panel of meringue, coconut coating—

you know what I mean.

Nor can you convince me
that popcorn machinery is not
the creator of brains,

piled high and dry, for sale  . . .

The children know what's going on:

one of them discovered
another hairpin function—

in a flash, the socket had him neon.

Such insight, the light of the times  . . .

Ecclesiastes, the Greek,
used to yell "Vanity! Vanity!"
like a dirty old man.

94

We knew what he wanted.

Now the kids chant "Commodity! Commodity!"
on their way to the five-and-ten.

His daughter drives a Buick named Electra.

They've come a ways since then  . . .

Saturdays, like occupation,
sirens and red lights
pace a parade through town.

Her Majesty sighs
from the back seats of convertibles—
where she spends her nights with fezzes—
vaselined, slick as nipples,
trailing taffy in her wake  . . .

A wake of cowboy boots and sideburns
bobbing, craning,
their trail scars
daubed mercurochrome like stigmata  . . .

Last Saturday, crazed,
one of them crashed a topless,
fashionable car into the procession.

It killed five Shriners and a twitching majorette.

Apprehended, nude,
he chewed his taffy like an addict.

His torso had been sprayed the latest shades;
his face with chicken dung.

His sequined penis seemed a razor in the sun.

They strapped him in plastic
and strung him up to die.

# Love, It Was

"Stop it!" she said, as I kissed her:
I was playing the white keys of her spine.
When she fell asleep I opened her back
with a pen knife—

the spine came, then the rest of the frame—

then set it to dry on its hands and knees.

When she awoke I was grooving the blues,
two pencils as mallets, in my blue bathrobe.

And she cried: "Please! My frame, please!"

To which I replied:

"See. See how I love you.
My love is so many forms of music,
intricate and beautiful.

"The next time allow me to finish the tune."

# Bandstand

The focus is youth—casual
stances on the ballroom floor.

The boys are smooth; the girls
stick out all over.

Every mother's son
calls the tune
and bodies snap into action,

slanting the best angles to the camera.

They have been carefully screened.

Outside, the dusk on Philadelphia . . .

Meanwhile, they reach their peak,
doing "The Hitchhiker" on national TV—

standing in place, thumbing a ride . . .

One of them, of course,
is Richard Speck—

he's in the corner of your screen—

having a blast,
dancing his ass off
with a teased little trick.

He got here early,
stashed his Mustang in the alley;
he'll probably get tagged
but who cares?—

He's got a part-time gig.
She finally accepted.
He's on the scene.

Then it's time for an ad—
some huge tube oozing out of itself  . . .

And ol' Dickie, cool
gum-popping Dickie,
struts it into the men's room

for a smoke, to contemplate
a pimple, to ponder whether to get a new
tattoo and join the Merchant Marines,
for kicks—

then makes it on out to join the music.

# Countries of War

It must be like being
postmaster, living
in a country of war.
The mail comes in:
addressee unknown.
The dead. More dead.
When your father dies,
you hide behind
the parcels, and cry.
Your brothers go:
one by one, canceled.
Your son is torn
open and scattered—
first limbs, an eye  .  .  .
Do you know this life?
When were *you* born?
I have always been
postmaster. Buy stamps.

# R and R in Bangkok

something about the eyes
going over my
shoulders up the slow
rise of grass
and giving back
something instead called
R and R in Bangkok

    buying without
    shopping much
    bargaining by
    paying the duration
    rubbing yourself
    numb on it
    washboard that
    does not wash
    same old song
    and trance
    sick kid sick
    something finally
    finding a thin
    hipped thin
    titted child beside
    you on a reeking
    beach

    sick tired

trading it
on a watch
watching the city
reel from a drunken
pagoda

sick flying

back to the same
sort of patrol

all that in these eyes
reciting what is
to be told as the afternoon
crashes off a watch
band bringing
ballrooms to these simple walls
in which there is
no crying
no laughing
no music
no dancing

# The Inada Report

None of that small stuff—
hair sights, and split-second timing—
all to fill the pages,
the pockets of controversy . . .

In my own commission,
through lifetime investigation,
after all my sights and frames,

I still have one question:

If there are so many blacks
slaving in the School Book Depository,
why are they not getting
closer than cartons

to books and to schools?

# Taxes and Ballots

He is the one
under a mountain—
tunnels and tubes.
You
cannot reach him.
Charlie McCarthy,
he is wood,
wired into city
offices.
He reaches you—
taxes and ballots,
policies
of wood.
What you must do
is move
into his offices.
He will feed you,
clothe you.
Do not speak.
He will hold you.
Swoon.

# The Tasting

You get tired of salt and pepper—
take out some Chinese food.

And I mean it's good, really—
wild spices, those relevant noodles  . . .

After you've eaten you take off your shoes.

The Red Guard runs wild as noodles.
They're ranting their ass off.

And old Chinamen used to
tie up a girl's foot,
sigh at the stump and croon:

"Man, that's groovy. That sure is good."

# For the E.H.W.

"How's the fruit this season?"
"Are you sure the set was on?"
"Are you sure you aren't Chester?"
"Don't you know Roy Wong?"

Well, this is my only answer:

There's a lot more of me
where I'm from, where I'm
continually being born;

and you have long red underwear
flagging out from under silk and tweed—
the secret uniform
of the Eternal Honkies of the World;

and one of these nights
when you're slipping into your
inside outhouse
and unbuttoning the flap,

I'm going to be there,
and, despite your drawl and twang,
there won't be any time

for questions *or* answers.

# Half Time at the Game

Come tip time, I was ready to wail.
WE jammed for a while,
played like a cage of clichés.

Then the OTHER got rough—
a big buck sweating like sex.
Saw his tail twitch.

So tossed a soft pun in the men's room
about THE championship race.

Then the Scouts came on,
moving like mobilization—
a strutting Mobil station—
hup-one, hup-one . . .
Lit a smoke. Put it out.
Took off my linty brim.

I knew it was coming,
the way they cut me up with glares
(forgot my brim at the NATIONAL ANTHEM).
The FIGHT SONG got me by surprise—
I forgot to rise,
hunching on the bench like a toilet bowl . . .

I remember better times.
Folks love me *because* I was a JAPO—

six-five, with all the moves.
Golden Goy, they called me—
the War over, my SUN on the rise.
I was a nine-sport man.
Had a whole smile of muscles.
Looked like a lot of yen.

Led the NATION, broke tapes,
folks looking for me like a contact lens.
Strode like a goalpost,
slick as a backboard,
numbers on my clothes like price tags.
And a dozen blondes
hugged me like a pom-pom,
tossing their panties at me for towels.
Ate five cheeseburgers
and a vase of fries.

They retired my name from the alphabet.

Then my head got heavy.
Took a scholar's ticket to Osprey Tech.
Played first sestina.
Made all NEW YORKER.
Formed a reading team called The Villanelles.
Toured the country with Prarie Cash,
the Grand Old Osprey.
Women on me like punctuation.

What else could I do?

So somebody stuck me in the Saturday Review.
Couldn't endorse a snowflake.
Nobody stealing my rhymes.
Kids quitting my old dropkick.

So here I am. Got nothing to do.
But there's a war coming up.
I'm gonna kick sand off the beachhead
at the Vietnamese.
And ol' GOD'S gotta light up like a scoreboard.

And when I get here again
I'll be the HALL OF FAME
in a blue blazer and wing-tip shoes.

Whoops.
Half time's over.
Gonna find me a phone booth and boo.

# Projected Scenario of a Performance to Be Given Before the U.N.

I am a mad mother-
fucker, or in other
words, a very irate
citizen—that's what
you call the black
and white of it all.
(general applause)
But that's an over-
simplification—how
about other colors?
(scattered applause)
And I'm supposed to
be yellow as butter
or expensive spread?
Call me a very irate
fatherhugger, that's
what we Asians have
to be, making these
various variations.
But, you fine folks
sitting there behind
smiles and earphones,
don't you know that
Yellow is now in THE
majority, according

to THE latest census?
Wake up—we are king
kong over this world.
And that's why I've
retired as uncrowned
undefeated Japanese
American myopic fast
draw $1.98 stickless
temporary press poet.
Nobody listened but
a listless literati.
I got better things
to do. Lot quicker.
Quicker than trivial
treaties or ass-pats
and some minor dying.
Nothing shaping up.
That's why I shaped
this up like a comb—
so turn it sideways—
isn't that the way
we write and screw?
(applause from Jap
and Chink delegates)
That's why I already
shipped this c.o.d.
hotline to all your
prexies and diplomats
and right about NOW
they're stroking at
that funky-butt hair
and splitting right
quick from multiple
yellow monosodium A-
sian flu and nuclear

mongoloid jaundice—
whoo whee yeah, man.
(very loud applause
from slanty sections,
plus ahsos and gongs,
what else but gongs)
I tried to make this
in Confucius' shape
so it could puff up
and fly way out and
he could snipe your
ass off—but that'd
take too much time.
Get the doors, Boys—
Numbers 5 to 18 Sons—
it's what's written,
it's all over, we're
taking over, taking
back fortune cookies,
eye operations, bug
juice. Taking over
Hollywood *and* EBONY.
Taking over your old
calendar. Last year
was Year of the Wasp.
And everybody's got
to eat noodley food
with pipe cleaners.
Toss me that kimono,
Boys, and my thongs.
Make sure it's Jap
slapped on the soles.
Everybody up, y'all.
Madame Butterfly Rag.
So all together now,

sing! Think Yellow!
Bonsai! Viva Banzai!
Top Bonanza! You're
in the yellow misce-
genation, number one
like a chinaman could
with liberty or chop-
sticks for all—Bong!

# That I Know

For Malcolm

. . . and I was smashed
into the gullet, daylight
bitten off behind.
Gashes where the claws
had clung, gullies
where the spit and blood
would run, pooling,
souring in ruts . . .

Then I was in the gut,
crushed with masses
in decay. Blind
in blackness, smothering . . .

To breathe then,
as I had never known.
To see then,
have sight to strike
with at the walls—
the feel of flesh
enough to make one
lash out without will . . .

Then light, finally,
down the gauntlet
of an alley—
where we must go.

Brothers, Sisters—
that I know.

And mostly in the bathroom—
that I know—
rising from the bowl
and glancing back, odor
on me like a skin,
luxuriant, beautiful—
that I know—

remembering fighting
out that slimy hole, loving
the validity of shit!

*The Stand*

# The Stand

I am somewhere
where I have decided to stand.

There has been long
maneuvering,

having been staked to a land,
sowing in the heat,

moving huge tools
in an absurdity of moon.

Chanting, my own
tune in the machinery,

I find the chanting soothes.
That sweet voice is ruined.

I move now,
sifting pavements through my feet,

sweat in the eyes, a horizon.
Sun turns the wheat.

Braced to my spine,
I resume the chanting—

utterances in a sound
octaves older than my own.

# The Journey

Miles was waiting on the dock,
his trumpet in a paper bag.

Lady was cold—
wind lashed the gardenias
I stole for her hair.

We were shabby, the three of us.

No one was coming so I started to row.

It was hard going—
stagnant, meandering . . .

The city moaned and smoldered.
Tin cans on the banks like shackles . . .

To be discovered, in the open . . .

But Miles took out his horn
and played.
Lady sang.

A slow traditional blues.

The current caught us—
horn, voice, oar stroking water . . .

I don't know how long we floated—

our craft so full of music,
the night so full of stars.

When I awoke we were entering an ocean,
sun low on water
warm as a throat,
gold as a trumpet.

We wept.

Then soared in a spiritual.

Never have I been so happy.

# The  Great  Bassist

For  Charles  Mingus

I am the Great Bassist:
music, life, are one.
And it is fine.

It wasn't always that way  . . .

When I was young,
music plugged my veins
and wouldn't run.

I bought a bass
and practiced.

Nothing would come:

wire
lanced the flesh only—
that ache inside,
unletting—

lacerations
of a master's whip
cutting
down through the calluses,
society in the cracks
like salt and pepper  . . .

Then bass was woman;
I, her master.

She was black, Africa's
shape
misshapened. We made
love like hate.
We bled
all over each other.
I plucked
her guts until we almost died  . . .

One night, I saw a light
shouldering the horizon—

a light we made.

It accompanied us.

And when the blues
came down like rain,
we played
away the rain,
and love fell
into place like syllogisms  . . .

The best of nights, we made
sea-rhythm, pulse
of wave strength
lapping sand.

Moon and earth, each
of the other, we strummed
telephone wires in a cold field—

music like blood
rushing, blood of all peoples,

humming, rushing . . .

I am in Levi's now—
that doesn't matter.

And when I walk the streets
wind
flattens my beard
and I look tired, tattered.

That doesn't matter.

But I need your love.
We need
each other.

So when I come down your street
with my Great Bass—

toss us your love—

we'll play you
love petals.

Love us back.

If you don't, we'll kill you.

All of you.

We will.

124